I0002246

BIM
FOR ARCHITECTURAL
FIRMS

BIM
FOR ARCHITECTURAL FIRMS

A Short Introduction

EDITOR **FAISAL U-K**

D&B Emerging Tech

a design technology company.

Copyright © 2023 by D AND B EMERGING TECH LIMITED d/b/a D&B Emerging Tech. All rights reserved.

BIM FOR ARCHITECTURAL FIRMS: A Short Introduction

First Edition

Published by D AND B EMERGING TECH LIMITED d/b/a D&B Emerging Tech.

All rights reserved. No part of this publication may be reproduced, distributed, or transmitted in any form or by any means, including photocopying, recording, or other electronic or mechanical methods, without the prior written permission of the publisher, except in the case of brief quotations embodied in critical reviews and certain other noncommercial uses permitted by copyright law.

The D&B Emerging Tech logo is a registered trademark of D AND B EMERGING TECH LIMITED.

ISBN: 979-8-3921-0339-3 (Paperback)
ASIN: B0C47NK3C6 (Paperback)
ASIN: B0C3FY534N (eBook)

Disclaimer:
The information in this book is provided "as is" without warranty of any kind. D AND B EMERGING TECH LIMITED and the authors make no representation or warranty, express or implied, including without limitation any warranties of merchantability, fitness for a particular purpose, or non-infringement. In no event shall D AND B EMERGING TECH LIMITED or the authors be liable for any damages whatsoever, including special, indirect, or consequential damages, arising out of or in connection with the use or inability to use the information in this book.

The information contained in this book is intended to be educational and not to be used for any specific purpose. The publisher, author, and any other third-party contributor to the book are not liable for any damages or injury caused by the use of or reliance on the information provided in the book. It is the responsibility of the reader to evaluate the information and to seek professional advice if needed. The views expressed in this book are those of the author and do not necessarily reflect the views of the publisher.

Cover photo by photographer Viktor Jakovlev.

Dedication

This book is dedicated to all the architects, engineers, and construction professionals who strive to make our built environment more efficient, sustainable, and beautiful through the use of Building Information Modeling. We hope this book provides valuable insights and inspiration for your continued work in the field.

Acknowledgments

We would like to express our gratitude to everyone who contributed to the creation of this book. Special thanks to our team at **D&B** Emerging Tech for their hard work and dedication in producing this guide. We also extend our appreciation to the professionals who generously shared their expertise and insights with us during the writing process.

Of course, a big thank you to Oliver Thomas, Design Technology Manager at Bjarke Ingels Group (BIG), for his invaluable contribution to this book and for writing the foreword. We would also like to thank Adam Stark, Co-Founder of Jet.Build, for his contributions.

Additionally, we would like to acknowledge the companies and organizations that have been a massive support throughout this process, including ARK, Archi-Tech Network (ATN), Pixel, Jet.Build, McNeel, and Autodesk. Finally we are also grateful to the International Organization for Standardization (ISO) for creating the ISO 19650 series, which has been an essential resource for this book. Thank you all for your work and for providing the resources that have helped shape this book.

Contents

List of Figures

List of Figures

Foreword by Oliver Thomas

Having spent the last 11 years of my career working in three global firms – Aedas, Front Inc., and Bjarke Ingels Group (BIG) – I have gained extensive experience in various aspects of Building Information Modeling (BIM) and its implementation during design stages and construction projects. Throughout my work on small-scale houses, large-scale commercial projects, and buildings with highly complex geometry, I have consistently witnessed the significant benefits of BIM. This powerful tool not only streamlines workflows and reduces time spent on drawing but also enhances value addition through improved design and critical thinking.

BIM has become an essential component of the design process for most practices in Europe and the US. As the Design Technology Manager at Bjarke Ingels Group, I have been supervising the integration of BIM into our design processes and projects. BIM has been a part of BIG's workflow for over a decade, contributing significantly to the firm's rapid growth and extensive construction achievements. Additionally, BIM has played a role in enhancing the commercial success of projects, as they are typically more profitable when utilizing BIM.

We employ BIM for various reasons, regardless of whether it is mandated by a client or the government. BIM streamlines our design process, extending beyond the conceptual stages. Utilizing Revit enables us to collaborate more efficiently in a coordinated environment, with teams working simultaneously on the same model in both 2D and 3D. This approach allows us to access more comprehensive information, avoiding issues that may arise from relying solely on 2D or 3D representations in later design stages.

Moreover, BIM facilitates higher levels of accuracy in internal and external coordination with consultants. The majority of our BIM projects are developed in collaboration with consultants, incorporating their models into ours. This integration allows us to address complex issues with far greater precision and detail.

Despite BIM being around for more than 20 years, its adoption in the industry has been slow, particularly in regions like Europe. This can be attributed to factors such as resistance to change and the learning curve associated with new software and workflows. However, once the initial investment in learning is made, most teams and individuals find the benefits of improved efficiency and documentation quality to be well worth the effort.

Revit, currently the most widely used BIM software, is my recommendation for practices looking to adopt BIM. As the industry continues to evolve, we anticipate the integration of game engines and AI into BIM platforms, which will make these tools even more user-friendly.

Recognizing the importance of technology adoption in the field of architecture, Faisal U-K, Guillaume Evain, and I founded the Archi-Tech Network (ATN) in 2021. ATN is an online platform aimed at fostering conversations about design and technology through podcasts, YouTube videos, and online courses. Our goal is to equip architects and students with the digital tools and technologies needed to become digitally fluent professionals.

BIM, being a crucial component of this, can be challenging to learn, but it is an invaluable skill to possess. To facilitate this, we have created a Revit Masterclass available at *https://archi-tech. network*. We also offer courses in computational design through Grasshopper and Rhino.Inside to introduce Computational BIM into your practice.

This book is designed to help you integrate BIM into your design process, regardless of the size or scale of your practice and projects. While the initial steps may seem daunting, this book will guide you through the implementation process, enabling you to quickly experience the advantages of incorporating BIM into your workflow.

Oliver Thomas
Bjarke Ingels Group

Figure 1:
Shanghai Tower by Gensler, image by photographer Moiz K. Malik.

Introduction

Introduction

Building Information Modeling (BIM) is a game-changing digital process that is transforming the architecture industry. At its core, BIM is a collaborative process that uses digital technology to create, manage, and share building information throughout the entire lifecycle of a project. It allows architects, engineers, contractors, and other building professionals to work together seamlessly, resulting in better designs, more efficient construction processes, and reduced costs.

BIM allows architects to create more accurate and detailed models of buildings, which helps them to identify and resolve potential issues earlier in the design process. This early detection of problems allows architects to make better design decisions and significantly reduces the number of errors that occur during construction. Moreover, BIM can improve communication and collaboration among project stakeholders, leading to increased efficiency and better project outcomes.

BIM has been in development for several decades, with early versions of the technology first emerging in the 1970s. However, it wasn't until the 1990s that BIM began to gain widespread acceptance in the architecture industry. Today, BIM has become the industry standard for building design and construction, and it is used by architects, engineers, contractors, and other building professionals all over the world.

Surveys indicate that companies that actively measure BIM ROI are experiencing significant returns, with initial ROIs ranging from 300% to 500%. A follow-up survey showed that firms that measured ROI perceived higher benefits than those that didn't. ROI can be measured in different ways, with firms tracking aspects such as project outcomes, improved communication, and a positive impact on winning projects. PCL Construction and Holder Construction are two examples of companies that have achieved significant ROI from BIM, with most of the payback coming from clash-detection efforts that greatly reduce costly change orders.

It is essential to note that BIM is not just a software or tool but a process that requires a shift in mindset and a willingness to embrace change. BIM adoption requires a commitment to ongoing education and training, as well as an investment in the right tools and software. However, the benefits of BIM adoption far outweigh the costs, making it a worthwhile investment for architectural firms looking to improve their project outcomes and remain competitive in the industry.

In this book, we will explore the various aspects of BIM adoption, including the benefits of using BIM in architecture, the tools and software available for BIM, the workflows and processes used in BIM, the standards and protocols associated with BIM, and the challenges and opportunities of BIM implementation and adoption. We will also examine case studies of successful BIM implementation in architectural firms and look at emerging trends and technologies in BIM.

Whether you are an architect looking to enhance your skills or an architectural firm looking to adopt BIM, this book will provide you with the essential information you need to get started with BIM and take advantage of the many benefits it offers. By the end of this book, you will have a thorough understanding of BIM and its applications in architectural firms, and you will be equipped with the knowledge to take the next step in BIM adoption.

Figure 2:
Burj Khalifa by Adrian Smith (Skidmore, Owings & Merrill), image by photographer Jeff Tumale.

Chapter 1: Benefits of BIM for Architectural Firms

1. Benefits of BIM for Architectural Firms

BIM is an indispensable tool for architectural firms looking to enhance their project delivery process. By utilizing BIM, architects can streamline their workflow and improve their communication and collaboration with other stakeholders in the project. The benefits of using BIM in architecture are numerous, and they include:

1.1. Improved Project Coordination and Communication

BIM enables architects to collaborate more effectively with other stakeholders involved in a project. With BIM, all project information is stored in a centralized database that can be accessed by all stakeholders, allowing for better communication and coordination throughout the project lifecycle. This reduces the risk of errors, omissions, and conflicts, and helps to ensure that all parties are working towards the same project goals.

1.2. Increased Accuracy and Efficiency in Project Design and Documentation

BIM provides architects with a more accurate and detailed representation of a building, enabling them to identify potential design issues earlier in the design process. This helps to minimize errors and rework, leading to greater efficiency and cost savings. BIM also makes it easier to produce high-quality documentation, such as construction drawings and specifications, which can be generated automatically from the BIM model.

1.3. Enhanced Visualization and Presentation Capabilities

BIM allows architects to create highly realistic and interactive visualizations of a building, enabling stakeholders to better understand the design and make more informed decisions. This can include 3D models, virtual reality simulations, and augmented reality experiences, which can be used to visualize the building in different contexts and scenarios.

1.4. Better Project Cost and Schedule Control

BIM can help architects to better control project costs and schedules by providing a more accurate and detailed understanding of the building design and construction process. This allows architects to identify potential cost and schedule risks earlier in the project lifecycle and to make informed decisions to mitigate these risks.

1.5. Improved Sustainability and Environmental Performance

BIM can help architects to design buildings that are more sustainable and environmentally friendly by providing tools and information for energy modeling, life cycle assessment, and other sustainability analyses. This allows architects to make informed decisions about building materials, systems, and technologies that can reduce the environmental impact of a building and improve its energy efficiency.

1.6. Faster and More Accurate Document Completion:

With BIM, architects can complete documents faster and with greater accuracy. This reduces the risk of errors and variations, as all the information is stored in one place, making it easier to retrieve and communicate to other stakeholders.

1.7. Improved Building Quality:

BIM enables architects to produce a fully coordinated design that takes into consideration all aspects of the building, from structure to systems. This leads to better building quality and reduces the risk of construction delays and rework.

1.8. Certainty of Project Cost and Completion Period:

BIM provides architects with a more accurate and detailed understanding of the building design and construction process, allowing them to identify potential cost and schedule risks earlier in the project lifecycle. This leads to greater certainty in project cost and completion period, which is crucial for the success of a project.

In summary, the benefits of BIM in architectural firms are numerous and far-reaching. By utilizing BIM, architects can improve their communication and collaboration, increase their accuracy and efficiency, enhance their visualization and presentation capabilities, better control project costs and schedules, design more sustainable buildings, and produce higher quality buildings. By incorporating BIM into their project delivery process, architectural firms can differentiate themselves in a highly competitive market and deliver better projects that meet the needs of their clients and stakeholders.

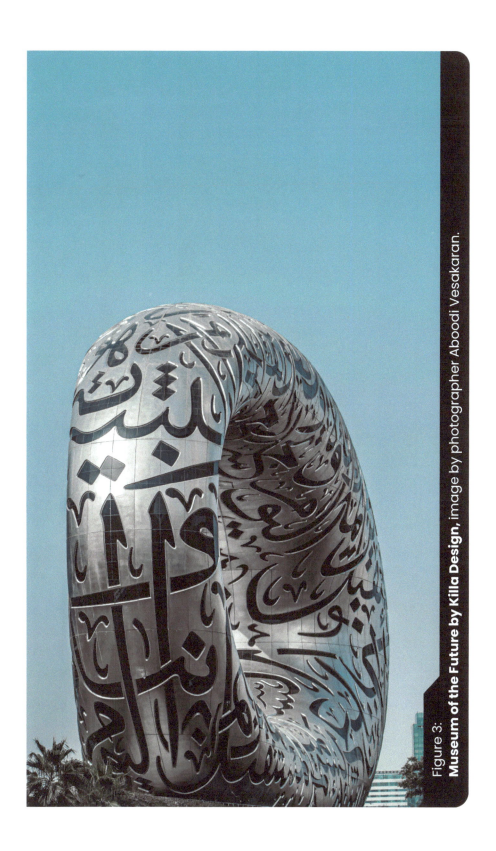

Figure 3:
Museum of the Future by Killa Design, image by photographer Aboodi Vesakaran.

Figure 4:
Plot 99, CBD, Abuja, Nigeria by D&B Ltd, image courtesy of D&B Ltd. ©

Chapter 2: Convincing Clients, Facility Managers, Contractors, and Consultants

2. Convincing Clients, Facility Managers, Contractors, and Consultants

BIM is a powerful tool that can help architects create more accurate designs, save time and money, and improve collaboration with other stakeholders involved in the construction process. However, the success of BIM implementation in an architectural firm depends on the buy-in from various stakeholders such as clients, facility managers, contractors, and consultants.

In this chapter, we will explore the reasons why it is crucial for architects to convince these stakeholders to adopt BIM. We will also provide insights on how architects can effectively communicate the benefits of BIM to each stakeholder group, and how they can tailor their approach to meet the specific needs of each group.

2.1. Clients

2.1.1. Why it is important to convince clients:

Convincing clients to adopt BIM is crucial for architects because it allows them to provide a more comprehensive and efficient service. BIM enables architects to create accurate 3D models, simulations, and visualizations that help clients better understand the design, resulting in better-informed decisions. BIM also allows architects to collaborate more effectively with clients and other stakeholders, resulting in better outcomes and a smoother project delivery.

2.1.2. How to convince clients:

To convince clients to adopt BIM, architects can highlight the benefits of using BIM, such as better visualization and understanding of the design, improved collaboration and communication, more accurate cost estimation, and reduced errors and rework. Architects can also showcase their experience and expertise in using BIM, demonstrate how it can improve the design process and project outcomes, and provide case studies or examples of previous projects where BIM was used successfully.

2.1.3. Benefits of BIM for clients:

- Improved visualization and understanding of the design: BIM allows architects to create accurate 3D models and simulations that help clients visualize and better understand the design, resulting in better-informed decisions and a higher degree of satisfaction with the final outcome.

- Improved collaboration and communication: BIM enables architects to collaborate more effectively with clients and other stakeholders, resulting in better communication and a smoother project delivery.

- More accurate cost estimation: BIM provides more accurate data and information that helps clients better estimate project costs, reducing the risk of cost overruns and delays.

- Reduced errors and rework: BIM allows architects to identify and resolve design issues early on, reducing the risk of errors and rework later in the project and saving clients time and money.

○ Faster project delivery: BIM enables architects to work more efficiently, reducing the time needed to complete the design and construction phases of the project, resulting in faster project delivery.

○ Improved sustainability: BIM can be used to optimize the design for energy efficiency, reducing energy consumption and costs for clients in the long run.

○ Increased project value: BIM can add value to a project by improving design quality, reducing risk, and enhancing collaboration and communication, resulting in a better outcome for clients.

○ Competitive advantage: Clients are increasingly looking for architects who are using BIM, as it provides a more efficient and comprehensive service. Using BIM can give architects a competitive advantage in the market.

○ Future-proofing: Adopting BIM now can future-proof a project and ensure that it is compatible with emerging technologies and practices, reducing the need for costly and time-consuming upgrades later on.

○ Improved facility management: BIM can be used to create accurate and detailed models of the building, providing clients with valuable information for facility management and maintenance.

2.2. Facility Managers

2.2.1.   Why it is important to convince Facility Managers:

Facility managers are responsible for ensuring the proper functioning and maintenance of a building's systems and equipment. By convincing facility managers to adopt BIM, architects can ensure that the building's design and construction are aligned with the goals of the facility management team, resulting in a more efficient and effective building. Additionally, BIM can help facility managers with maintenance and repairs by providing accurate and up-to-date information about the building's systems and equipment.

2.2.2.   How to convince Facility Managers:

To convince facility managers to adopt BIM, architects can demonstrate the benefits of BIM for facility management, such as improved efficiency and reduced maintenance costs. Architects can also emphasize that BIM can provide facility managers with accurate and up-to-date information about the building's systems and equipment, which can help them plan and prioritize maintenance and repairs.

2.2.3.   Benefits of BIM for Facility Managers:

○   Improved building efficiency: BIM can help Facility Managers optimize building systems and operations, leading to improved energy efficiency and reduced waste.

○   Reduced maintenance costs: BIM provides accurate and up-to-date information about building systems and equipment, helping Facility Managers identify potential maintenance issues before they become major problems, ultimately reducing costs.

○ Accurate and up-to-date information about building systems and equipment: BIM provides detailed and accurate information about building systems, equipment, and assets, allowing Facility Managers to better understand and manage their facilities.

○ Improved planning and prioritization of maintenance and repairs: BIM helps Facility Managers prioritize maintenance and repairs based on the criticality of building systems and equipment, ensuring that resources are allocated effectively.

○ Improved communication and collaboration with design and construction teams: BIM enables Facility Managers to communicate more effectively with design and construction teams during the planning and construction phases, resulting in better building designs and smoother handovers.

○ Enhanced ability to identify and address potential issues before they become major problems: BIM provides Facility Managers with the ability to identify potential issues and address them proactively, reducing downtime and improving building performance.

○ Increased transparency and accountability in building operations: BIM can improve transparency and accountability by providing accurate and up-to-date information about building systems and operations to all stakeholders.

○ Improved ability to track and manage energy usage and costs: BIM can help Facility Managers track and analyze energy usage and costs, allowing them to identify areas for improvement and implement energy-saving strategies.

○ Enhanced ability to plan and implement sustainability initiatives: BIM provides Facility Managers with the ability to model and simulate different sustainability scenarios, helping them make informed decisions about sustainability initiatives.

○ Improved ability to manage building data and analytics: BIM enables Facility Managers to centralize and manage building data and analytics, making it easier to access and analyze information to inform decision-making.

2.3. Contractors

2.3.1.   Why it is important to convince Contractors:

Contractors are essential stakeholders in the construction process, responsible for executing designs and ensuring that projects are completed on time and within budget. Convincing contractors to use BIM can improve collaboration, reduce conflicts and errors, and ultimately result in a better quality product.

2.3.2.   How to convince Contractors:

To convince contractors to adopt BIM, architects can highlight the benefits of improved communication, reduced conflicts and errors, and the ability to detect clashes and resolve them before construction begins. Architects can also demonstrate how BIM can help streamline the construction process, reduce rework, and improve the accuracy of cost estimates.

2.3.3. Benefits of BIM for Contractors:

○ Increased efficiency in construction process: BIM enables contractors to streamline the construction process by providing accurate and up-to-date information, reducing the need for manual coordination, and facilitating collaboration between teams.

○ Improved communication and collaboration with design and engineering teams: BIM promotes communication and collaboration between contractors, designers, and engineers, allowing for seamless project integration, quick problem solving, and efficient decision-making.

○ Reduced conflicts and errors during construction: By providing a comprehensive overview of the project, BIM helps contractors to identify potential conflicts and errors before construction begins, reducing the risk of project delays and costly rework.

○ Enhanced ability to detect and resolve clashes before construction begins: BIM enables contractors to identify and resolve clashes between building systems

and components before construction begins, reducing the risk of rework and costly
delays.

○ Improved accuracy of cost estimates: BIM
allows contractors to create accurate and
detailed cost estimates based on the most
up-to-date information, improving project planning and reducing the risk of cost
overruns.

○ Streamlined change order management:
BIM enables contractors to quickly and
easily manage change orders, ensuring
that all project stakeholders are kept up-
to-date with the latest information.

○ Enhanced ability to plan and schedule
construction activities: BIM provides contractors with a comprehensive view of the
project, enabling them to plan and schedule construction activities more effectively,
reducing project duration and cost.

○ Improved safety through better visualization of construction processes: BIM provides
contractors with a better understanding of
the construction process, enabling them to
identify potential safety hazards and implement appropriate safety measures.

○ Improved ability to manage and track materials and resources: BIM enables contractors to manage and track materials
and resources more effectively, reducing
waste, improving efficiency, and reducing
costs.

○ Improved ability to identify and address

potential issues before they become major problems: By providing a comprehensive view of the project, BIM enables contractors to identify potential issues early on, reducing the risk of major problems and costly rework.

2.4. Consultants

2.4.1.   Why it is important to convince Consultants:

Consultants play a crucial role in the construction industry. They are experts in their field and provide specialized knowledge and advice to architects, engineers, and contractors. Converting consultants to BIM can lead to a more efficient and effective project management process. It is important to convince consultants to adopt BIM because it can improve the overall quality of a project and provide a competitive advantage for firms.

2.4.2.   How to convince Consultants:

To convince consultants to adopt BIM, it is important to demonstrate the benefits that BIM can offer to their work. Showing them successful case studies of similar projects that have used BIM can be a persuasive technique. Another strategy is to invite them to BIM workshops or training sessions to learn about the benefits of BIM and see how it can improve their work. Providing support and guidance during the adoption process can also help to convince consultants to integrate BIM into their workflow.

2.4.3. Benefits of BIM for Consultants:

○ Improved collaboration and communication with design and construction teams: BIM allows consultants to work collaboratively with other stakeholders by sharing and exchanging project data. This improved communication streamlines the decision-making process and ensures that all parties are working towards the same goals.

○ Improved efficiency and accuracy of project management: BIM can help consultants to manage their projects more efficiently by providing real-time project information and allowing for better analysis of design options. This can lead to more accurate cost estimates and better resource management.

○ Enhanced ability to analyze and mitigate project risks: BIM provides consultants with the ability to identify and mitigate risks early on in the design and construction process. This can lead to better project outcomes, reduced project delays, and lower overall costs.

○ Improved ability to manage project data and analytics: BIM provides a centralized location for all project data, making it easier for consultants to manage and analyze project information. This can lead to improved project insights and better decision-making.

○ Enhanced ability to design and implement sustainable solutions: BIM allows consultants to analyze and test different design options and scenarios to determine the most sustainable solution. This can lead to reduced environmental impact and improved long-term cost savings.

○ Improved ability to deliver high-quality projects on time and on budget: By using BIM, consultants can better plan and manage their projects, leading to higher quality projects that are delivered on time and on budget.

○ Improved ability to win new business and gain a competitive advantage: As more firms adopt BIM, it is becoming increasingly important for consultants to have BIM capabilities in order to remain competitive and win new business.

○ Improved ability to attract and retain talent: Younger generations of consultants are increasingly interested in working with advanced technology, including BIM. By adopting BIM, firms can attract and retain top talent in their field.

○ Enhanced ability to offer innovative solutions to clients: BIM provides consultants with a platform to create and test innovative design solutions, leading to more creative and unique projects.

○ Improved ability to deliver projects that meet client expectations: By using BIM, consultants can better understand and meet their clients' expectations, leading to higher client satisfaction and repeat business.

In conclusion, convincing clients, facility managers, contractors, and consultants to use BIM is essential for the success of any architectural project. By highlighting the benefits of BIM and showing stakeholders how BIM can help them achieve their goals, architects can improve the chances of BIM adoption and improve the overall success of the project.

As the architectural industry continues to evolve and adapt to new technologies, it is crucial for architects to embrace and utilize tools like BIM to stay competitive and provide the best possible service to their clients. By educating themselves and their stakeholders on the benefits of BIM, architects can position themselves as leaders in the industry and drive the adoption of this powerful technology.

Figure 5: **3D modeling office workspace**, image by photographer Sigmund.

Chapter 3: Implementing BIM in Architectural Firms

3. Implementing BIM in Architectural Firms

Implementing BIM can be a challenging process, but the benefits it offers are worth the effort. In this chapter, we'll provide a step-by-step guide to implementing BIM in your architectural firm.

3.1. Assess Your Needs and Resources

The first step in implementing BIM is to assess your firm's needs and resources. Determine your firm's BIM goals and what you hope to achieve by using BIM. This will help you identify the BIM software and hardware that best suit your firm's needs and budget. Additionally, consider the level of training and education your staff will need to successfully adopt BIM.

3.2. Develop a BIM Execution Plan (BEP)

A BIM Execution Plan (BEP) is a roadmap for implementing BIM on a specific project. It outlines the processes and procedures that will be used throughout the project and ensures that everyone involved in the project is working collaboratively towards the same goals. Developing a BEP will help you identify potential issues and challenges and develop strategies to overcome them.

3.3. Choose the Right BIM Software and Hardware

Choosing the right BIM software and hardware is critical to the success of your BIM implementation. There are many different BIM software options available, each with its own strengths and weaknesses. Consider your firm's budget, BIM goals, and staff expertise when selecting a BIM software. Additionally, make sure that the hardware you select is capable of running the software effectively.

3.4. Train Your Staff

BIM requires a new way of working, so it's essential that your staff receives proper training and education. This will help them understand the new processes and procedures involved in using BIM and develop the skills they need to use the software effectively. Consider providing both formal training sessions and on-the-job training to ensure that your staff is comfortable using the software.

3.5. Establish BIM Standards and Guidelines

Developing BIM standards and guidelines is an important step in ensuring that everyone in your firm is using BIM consistently and effectively. BIM standards and guidelines should cover all aspects of BIM, from software and hardware to processes and procedures. They should be regularly reviewed and updated to reflect changes in your firm's BIM goals and the latest industry best practices.

3.6. Implement Best Practices for BIM Project Management

Effective project management is critical to the success of any BIM project. Develop best practices for managing BIM projects, including collaboration, communication, and quality control. Use these best practices throughout the project to ensure that everyone is working collaboratively towards the same goals and that the project stays on track.

Architectural firms can benefit from implementing BIM, but it can be a challenging process. To successfully implement BIM, it is recommended that architects embrace the Level of Development initiative and project contracting methods. This helps define consistent inter-party deliverables, which can help architects engage more fully in model sharing, something they currently do least frequently. Architects should also focus on longer-term benefits, such as productivity and repeat business, to improve ROI. The benefits of BIM are not always immediately apparent to architects, but research indicates that contractors receive benefits more quickly than architects.

For non-users, research findings should be used to set appropriate expectations for getting started with BIM. It is also recommended that non-users look to BIM users at higher levels to help establish goals for the path forward.

Overall, the benefits of BIM are worth the effort required to implement it. By following the steps outlined in this chapter, architectural firms can successfully implement BIM, achieve their goals, and take advantage of the many benefits it offers.

Figure 6:
Autodesk Revit model, image by photographer Evgeniy Surzhan.

Figure 7:
Construction project in Calgary Alberta, Canada, image by photographer Ryunosuke Kikuno.

Chapter 4: The Challenge of Building Without BIM

4. The Challenge of Building Without BIM

As architecture firms continue to rely on traditional analogue and outdated practices, the challenge of building without Building Information Modeling (BIM) is becoming increasingly apparent. The use of multiple documents that are manually produced and coordinated is an inefficient and costly practice that is prone to human error and duplication of efforts. These inefficiencies often lead to abortive works, excessive checking, and delays in the project lifecycle.

The highly fragmented nature of the building industry involving many stakeholders at different stages of the project lifecycle has made the traditional approach to building information management challenging. The current building information 'devices' that are being used such as 2D drawings, spreadsheets, and documents are not only inefficient but are also prone to inconsistencies and errors.

BIM technology addresses these challenges by providing a single digital platform for collaboration, coordination, and management of the building information. BIM modeling replaces analogue methods of designing and documenting buildings, providing a more efficient, accurate, and cost-effective way of managing building information.

With BIM, project teams can work collaboratively in a shared model, ensuring that all stakeholders have access to the latest information. This digital platform reduces the time and costs associated with traditional analogue practices, minimizing the risks of abortive works and reducing the need for excessive checking.

BIM offers architecture firms a competitive edge by streamlining the project lifecycle, reducing errors, and enhancing coordination between stakeholders. By adopting BIM technology, firms can save costs and time while improving the quality and accuracy of their projects.

In conclusion, the challenges of building without BIM are becoming more apparent as traditional analogue practices become increasingly outdated. Architecture firms that have not yet adopted BIM technology risk falling behind their competitors in terms of efficiency, accuracy, and cost-effectiveness. BIM offers architecture firms a competitive edge by streamlining the project lifecycle, reducing errors, and enhancing coordination between stakeholders. It is time for firms to take advantage of BIM technology to improve their workflow and project outcomes.

Figure 8:
Demolition of Capital Plaza Office Tower, image by photographer Micah Williams.

Chapter 5: The Negative Impact of Not Using BIM

5. The Negative Impact of Not Using BIM

Imagine an architectural firm that once resisted embracing Building Information Modeling (BIM) technology. Projects were riddled with inefficiencies, delays, and soaring costs. Misunderstandings among stakeholders led to costly mistakes, and disputes became a common occurrence. But then, the firm decided to embrace BIM, and everything changed. This is not just a hypothetical scenario; it's a glimpse into the transformative power of BIM in the world of architecture. In this chapter, we'll explore the tangible and often costly negative impacts architectural firms face when they choose not to adopt BIM. By understanding these challenges, you'll gain valuable insights into why BIM is not merely an option but a necessity in the modern architectural landscape.

5.1. Duplication of Efforts

Without BIM, project teams are forced to work with multiple documents that need to be manually produced and coordinated, leading to duplication of efforts. This results in a significant waste of time and resources, as each document needs to be updated manually every time a change is made.

5.2. Disconnected Workflows

Traditional methods of building information management are highly fragmented, involving many stakeholders at different stages of the project lifecycle. This often leads to disconnected workflows and information, as information is not being shared in real-time between stakeholders.

5.3. Uncoordinated Information

Manual coordination of project information is time-consuming and prone to human error. This can result in uncoordinated information being used in the project, leading to misunderstandings, abortive work, re-work, and wasted materials.

5.4. Poor Communication

Poor communication can lead to delays, cost overruns, and disputes. Without a collaborative platform like BIM, communication between stakeholders can be slow and inefficient, resulting in missed deadlines and increased costs.

5.5. Misunderstandings

Misunderstandings can arise from different interpretations of drawings and specifications, leading to costly mistakes and delays in the construction process. BIM ensures that all stakeholders are working from the same information, reducing the risk of misunderstandings.

5.6. Re-work

Re-work, where work needs to be done again due to poor quality, can result in significant delays and additional costs. BIM helps reduce the risk of re-work by providing real-time quality control and ensuring that all stakeholders are working from the same information.

5.7. Wasted Materials

Wasted materials can occur due to poor planning or errors in the construction process. BIM helps reduce the risk of wasted materials by providing accurate and up-to-date information to all stakeholders, ensuring that the construction process is efficient and cost-effective.

5.8. Delays

Delays in the construction process can occur due to poor communication, misunderstandings, abortive work, re-work, and other factors. BIM helps reduce the risk of delays by providing a collaborative platform that ensures all stakeholders are working from the same information and collaborating in real-time.

5.9. Cost Overruns

Cost overruns can occur due to poor planning, delays, re-work, and other factors. BIM helps reduce the risk of cost overruns by providing accurate and up-to-date information to all stakeholders, ensuring that the construction process is efficient and cost-effective.

5.10. Dispute and Litigation

Disputes and litigation can arise due to misunderstandings, errors, delays, and other factors. BIM helps reduce the risk of disputes and litigation by providing a collaborative platform that ensures all stakeholders are working from the same information and collaborating in real-time.

By not implementing BIM in your architectural firm, you risk facing these negative impacts, which can result in wasted time, materials, and money. However, by adopting BIM, you can reduce the risk of these negative impacts and take advantage of the many benefits that BIM has to offer.

Figure 9:
Rundown high-rise in Bochum, Deutschland, image by photographer Mika Baumeister.

Figure 10: **Construction project in Buenos Aires, Argentina,** image by photographer Matías Santana.

Chapter 6: ROI of BIM for Architectural Firms

6. ROI of BIM for Architectural Firms

In this chapter, we will discuss the potential return on investment (ROI) of implementing BIM in your architectural firm. By providing real figures and examples, we hope to give you a better understanding of the costs and benefits of using BIM.

ROI is a critical factor in determining the financial success of a project. In the case of BIM, ROI is essential to evaluate its value for architectural firms. The results from surveys indicate that 48% of respondents are tracking BIM ROI at a moderate level or above. Moreover, companies that are actively measuring BIM ROI are experiencing initial ROIs ranging from 300 to 500%. (PCL Construction Case Study and Holder Construction interview). These numbers are significant and demonstrate the immense value that BIM can bring to architectural firms.

6.1. Cost of Implementing BIM

The costs associated with implementing BIM in an architectural firm can vary widely depending on the scope and complexity of the projects being undertaken. Typical costs include software, hardware, and training expenses.

For example, Autodesk Revit 2023, one of the leading BIM software programs, costs approximately $2,545 per year per user, although the complete AEC Collection costs approximately $3,430 per year per user, and BIM Collaborate Pro costs approximately $945 per year per user. Other costs to consider include the cost of training, which can range from $500 to $2,500 per person (depending on multiple factors including country, course format, duration, expertise, etc.). Lastly, the cost of hardware upgrades or new hardware, which can range from a few hundred to several thousand dollars.

6.2. Returns on Investment

A survey of AGC BIM Forum members conducted by McGraw-Hill Construction in November 2008 found that the average perception of ROI on BIM ranged from 11% to 30%. However, those who were actively measuring BIM ROI perceived a higher value. Among those measuring ROI, almost one-third reported an ROI greater than 100%, with several greater than 1,000%. These results demonstrate that measuring ROI establishes greater benefits from BIM than mere intuition suggests.

BIM ROI can be measured in different ways, and firms track different aspects of it. For instance, 79% of respondents indicated that BIM improves project outcomes, such as fewer requests for information (RFIs) and field coordination problems. Additionally, 79% said that BIM facilitates better communication due to 3D visualization, while 66% reported a positive impact on winning projects.

PCL Construction's case study is a prime example of how BIM ROI can be achieved. The company estimates that it is realizing a 500% ROI from BIM, with most of the payback coming from clash-detection efforts that greatly reduce costly change orders. Although the company realizes additional benefits that aren't calculated into ROI, such as saving time and effort, which is hard to quantify, PCL Construction proves that BIM can be an excellent investment.

Holder Construction Company is another example of a company that is actively measuring ROI on BIM projects. Michael LeFevre, Vice President of Planning

& Design, indicated that they have been using BIM since 2005, and during the first year, they were still developing the modeling skills and deciding on what metrics to track. Most of their tracking data is from 2006 forward, and they are gathering and using BIM metrics on many of their projects.

In conclusion, measuring BIM ROI is critical for determining the value that it brings to architectural firms. Companies that measure BIM ROI are experiencing significant returns, with initial ROIs ranging from 300 to 500%. Furthermore, measuring ROI establishes greater benefits from BIM than mere intuition suggests, as evidenced by survey results. The value of BIM ROI is proven, and companies that invest in it can reap significant benefits, including improved project outcomes, better communication, and a positive impact on winning projects.

Figure 11:
Construction project in Beijing, China, image by photographer Dylann Hendricks.

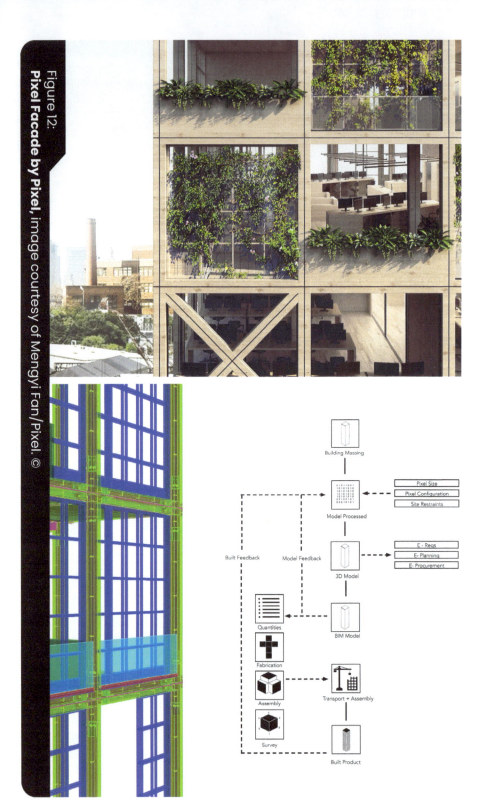

Figure 12:
Pixel Facade by Pixel, image courtesy of Mengyi Fan/Pixel. ©

Building Massing

Pixel Size
Pixel Configuration
Site Restraints

Model Processed

E - Regs
E- Planning
E- Procurement

3D Model

Built Feedback

Model Feedback

Quantities

BIM Model

Fabrication

Assembly

Transport + Assembly

Survey

Built Product

Chapter 7: Case Studies of Successful BIM Implementation in Architectural Firms

7. Case Studies of Successful BIM Implementation in Architectural Firms

Real-life case studies of successful BIM implementation in architectural firms provide valuable insights and lessons learned for other firms considering adopting BIM. This chapter highlights some examples of firms that have successfully implemented BIM and the benefits they have realized.

7.1. Case Study 1: HOK

HOK is an architectural firm that has implemented BIM to improve project delivery and collaboration. By using BIM, HOK has been able to improve project scheduling and reduce errors and rework. HOK has also used BIM to improve collaboration between project team members, resulting in better communication and fewer conflicts.

7.2. Case Study 2: Morphosis

Morphosis is an architectural firm founded in 1972 by Thom Mayne, who is also a Pritzker Prize-winning architect. The firm is known for its innovative designs and has worked on several high-profile projects such as the Perot Museum of Nature and Science in Dallas, Texas. The majority of the practice's projects are still typically organized in a design-bid-build process for contracts, meaning the deliverables are still two-dimensional documents derived from three-dimensional models that are tendered to the client and the contractor and subcontractors. However, the practice continues to rely heavily on two-dimensional drawings to ensure that they cover the required scope of work. They use the 2-D drawing set as a way of mitigating their own risk.

As part of their services, Morphosis provides

a three-dimensional model for information purposes. The practice has an early tendency to produce digital structural steel models in-house. As consulting engineers have more fully adopted BIM platforms, the practice now provides the technical consultants with a digital model as a basis for their scope of work. For facade development, the design team will provide the facade consultant with the parametric three-dimensional model for the design surface and the facade patterning scheme to be used as a reference for starting their own model. The Morphosis model is not used for fabrication; rather, this is a way for the practice to separate liabilities among the design team as all consultants are required to build their model. Each consultant models their BIM differently based on their own scope of work; however, model sharing ensures that a consultant does not have to start a new model from a two-dimensional set of drawings.

In the mid-1990s, the practice's original Director of Technology, Marty Doscher, was already pushing the office in a digital direction. On projects such as Caltrans District 7 Headquarters in Los Angeles, the practice had embarked on three-dimensional development processes. For that project, a 3-D model was used for the coordination of many trades; specifically, by overlaying digital CAD drawings on the structural steel model and looking for any discrepancies, the design team was bypassing the traditional shop drawing review process. Caltrans was being developed in 1997, and construction was ultimately completed in 2004. The building is important because it is a good example of Morphosis's desire to use digital tools to protect its design intent – in many of their projects, the structural steel is exposed in what Brugger described as the 'backend tectonic side of the building.' Ensuring a level of control to achieve that level of architectural intent ensures the building aesthetics and ultimately the quality of the architecture.

Morphosis continues to use various parametric tools such as Grasshopper and Bentley Systems' MicroStation®. Morphosis also uses GenerativeComponents (GC), the generative design suite that is now integrated with their BIM software. The practice continues to use GC as well as other parametric tools such as Grasshopper to study facade patterning, and generally, the choice of tool is dictated by project staffing. For larger parametric design problems, such as the Phare Tower in Paris, the practice is more commonly using Gehry Technologies' Digital Project.

7.3. Case Study 3: Gensler

Gensler is a firm that embraces the potential for digital technology to improve their design process, with the architect's role now involving the establishment of project parameters that can be embedded in the model. Gensler combines analogue and digital methods, with designers still sketching design intent manually, but also generating parameters to be used in an information model. This hybrid approach allows for a range of solutions to be created. Gensler has been exploring the use of supercomputers to render buildings in real-time in a three-dimensional view, to augment an already wide range of modeling and imaging tools.

The Shanghai Tower is the tallest building in Asia, and the design team used simulation to gauge the overall performance of the building in terms of lateral resistance to wind speed, and how the overall design and form of the building evolved due to lateral loading and other factors such as light reflectance. The building ultimately evolved with the vertical box form as the core and the most efficient shape for the floor plates around it being a circle. The building was enclosed by a double skin that circumscribed the circular floor plates with a series of triangles to account for the twisting the design team had originally intended for the tower. The team combined modeling and simulation within the computer and wind tunnel testing of physical models to generate these ideas.

The geometry of the Shanghai Tower became so complex it defied hand sketching and was only possible to visualize it with digital tools. The design team settled on approximately one degree of twist per floor, so over the original 121 floors there is about 120 degrees. Wind forces are the largest magnitude forces on the structure of a tower, and the design team returned to the concept of vortex shedding, understanding that there would be structural benefits to a geometric configuration that shed wind efficiently. The final design is highly efficient, with all the geometric expressiveness of the form achieved through the second layer of facade.

7.4. Case Study 4: A&Q Partnership

A&Q Partnership's Eight Gardens at Watford is a project aiming to deliver over 1,200 new homes to the area. With various consultants on the project at different levels of experience with BIM, some not as familiar with BIM workflows as A&Q Partnership, the initial appointments did not formally stipulate a BIM workflow. However, the teams were keen on developing the way they work and so agreed to proceed as a BIM project even though it wasn't obligatory. The team set expectations for each other and followed through with a tight execution plan. A&Q Partnership worked with DWG files and IFC files by referencing them into Vectorworks. The project shows how a collaborative approach to BIM can benefit even those parties who are less familiar with the process.

7.5. Case Study 5: Pixel

As architects we typically create bespoke solutions to bespoke problems, the AEC industry is one of the few to take this approach to creating a product. As a result the process of designing and building is extremely expensive and slow. The approach to this project takes a progressive attitude to create an adaptive, scalable, repeatable building system that can be configured to create multiple solutions that can be applied to multiple building typologies.

The Pixel Facade project ("Figure 12:" on page 58) utilized the combination of BIM, Computation and Modular Manufactured building components. We used computation to build a design configurator that can create assemblies that are unique to the local conditions of the site. BIM is utilized to detail, refine and document the building configuration using automation as much as possible. Each modular component is a BIM element with all the information need to fabricate, quantify and assemble the configuration of that particular building.

7.6. Case Study 6: Ittenbrechbühl

In designing the headquarters of Scott Sports, IttenBrechbühl used Vectorworks Architect's BIM processes to create a forward-looking, precise design based on improved communication and coordination among all stakeholders involved in the process. The use of 3D models allowed for coordinated naming and structure of levels and classes, stories, the definition of the project's origin, and the handling of IFC data, as well as wall and door styles and symbols. This lead to successful BIM collaboration. BIM communication via models was the key to the success of the project, which avoided misunderstandings that can arise from 2D drawings. The project highlights how BIM can help firms to collaborate and design more effectively.

7.7. Case Study 7: Flansburgh Architects

Flansburgh Architects specializes in educational architecture and used a BIM workflow for the design of a school for the town of Holbrook, Massachusetts. The firm previously used BIM among its internal design team for architectural documentation and coordination but needed a BIM-centric process to work effectively with external contractors and consultants. The firm built upon past experience and aimed to take the BIM process another step further with every new project. The biggest selling point for working in BIM was the fact that there can be one collaborative model with multiple kinds of data attached to it. Flansburgh Architects did their architectural design in Vectorworks, then used IFC to import, export, and reference files from all the consultants and subcontractors. The project shows that BIM workflows work best when data exchange is free and open, allowing all stakeholders to work in the software they prefer.

In conclusion, the case studies of successful BIM implementation in architectural firms highlight the benefits that firms can realize when they adopt BIM. HOK has been able to improve project scheduling and reduce errors and rework by using BIM. Morphosis, despite still relying on two-dimensional drawings, has successfully integrated BIM with various parametric tools to study facade patterning, and to protect their design intent. Gensler combines analogue and digital methods and has been exploring the use of supercomputers to render buildings in real-time in a three-dimensional view, to augment an already wide range of modelling and imaging tools. The case studies show that BIM can improve collaboration between project team members, result in better communication, and lead to the creation of more innovative designs. Adopting BIM is essential for firms that want to remain competitive and offer better services to their clients. By embracing BIM, architectural firms can achieve better project delivery, reduce errors, and create more value for their clients.

Figure 13:
30 St Mary Axe (The Gherkin) by Foster + Partners, image by photographer Viktor Forgacs.

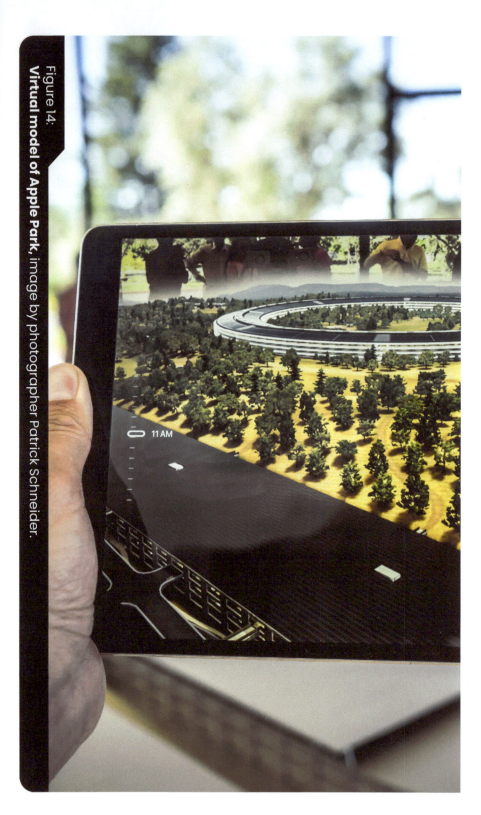

Figure 14:
Virtual model of Apple Park, image by photographer Patrick Schneider.

Chapter 8: Lessons Learned and Best Practices

8. Lessons Learned and Best Practices

Real-life case studies of successful BIM implementation in architectural firms provide valuable insights and lessons learned for other firms considering adopting BIM. The following are lessons learned and best practices from some examples of firms that have successfully implemented BIM:

8.1. Lesson 1: Improved Project Delivery and Collaboration

HOK, an architectural firm, has implemented BIM to improve project delivery and collaboration. By using BIM, HOK has been able to improve project scheduling and reduce errors and rework. HOK has also used BIM to improve collaboration between project team members, resulting in better communication and fewer conflicts.

8.2. Lesson 2: Using Digital Tools to Protect Design Intent

Morphosis, an architectural firm, has used digital tools to protect its design intent. For many of their projects, the structural steel is exposed in what the firm describes as the 'backend tectonic side of the building.' Ensuring a level of control to achieve that level of architectural intent ensures the building aesthetics and ultimately the quality of the architecture. The firm continues to use various parametric tools such as Grasshopper and Bentley Systems' MicroStation® to study facade patterning.

8.3. Lesson 3: Embracing Digital Technology to Improve the Design Process

Gensler, an architectural firm, embraces the potential for digital technology to improve its design process. Gensler combines analogue and digital methods, with designers still sketching design intent manually, but also generating parameters to be used in an information model. This hybrid approach allows for a range of solutions to be created. Gensler has also explored the use of supercomputers to render buildings in real-time in a three-dimensional view, to augment an already wide range of modelling and imaging tools.

8.4. Best Practice 1: Methodology

The case studies highlighted in the previous chapter offer valuable insights and lessons learned for firms considering implementing BIM. Key best practices include starting with a pilot project to test BIM implementation before scaling up to larger projects, investing in staff training and education to ensure they have the necessary skills and knowledge to use BIM effectively, developing project standards and protocols to ensure consistency and interoperability across projects and teams, establishing clear communication channels and workflows to ensure effective collaboration and coordination between project team members, and regularly reviewing and evaluating project progress to identify areas for improvement and adjust project workflows and processes as needed.

8.5. Best Practice 2: Establish Project Parameters in the Model

Gensler's approach involves establishing project parameters that can be embedded in the model. This approach ensures that the design team can gauge the overall performance of the building in terms of lateral resistance to wind speed and other factors, such as light reflectance.

8.6. Best Practice 3: Combine Modelling and Simulation

The design team for the Shanghai Tower, the tallest building in Asia, combined modelling and simulation within the computer and wind tunnel testing of physical models to generate ideas. The building ultimately evolved with the vertical box form as the core and the most efficient shape for the floor plates around it being a circle. The building was enclosed by a double skin that circumscribed the circular floor plates with a series of triangles to account for the twisting the design team had originally intended for the tower.

In conclusion, BIM implementation provides architectural firms with numerous benefits, including improved project delivery, better communication, and fewer conflicts. To adopt BIM successfully, firms must embrace digital technology and combine modelling and simulation within the computer and wind tunnel testing of physical models to generate ideas. Establishing project parameters in the model ensures that the design team can gauge the overall performance of the building in terms of lateral resistance to wind speed and other factors, such as light reflectance. Lastly, firms should use digital tools to protect their design intent and ensure building aesthetics and ultimately the quality of the architecture.

Figure 15:
The Shard by Renzo Piano, image by photographer C. Valdez.

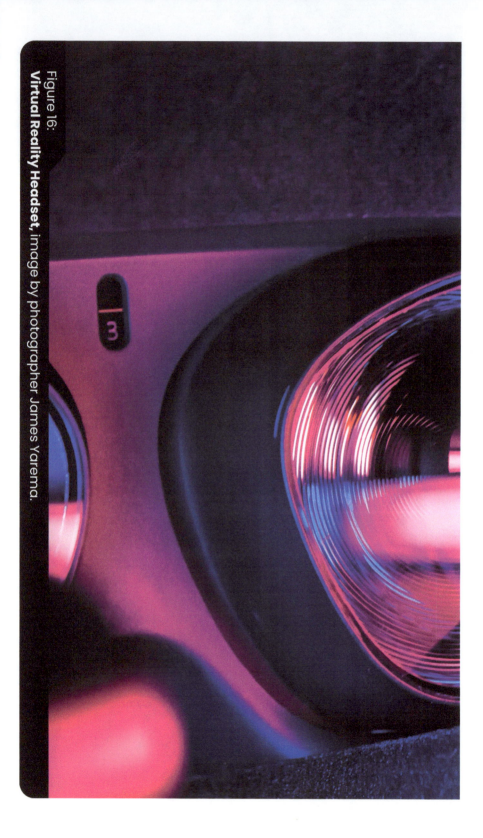

Figure 16: **Virtual Reality Headset,** image by photographer James Yarema.

Chapter 9: Future of BIM in Architectural Firms

9. Future of BIM in Architectural Firms

As technology advances, the use of Building Information Modeling (BIM) in architectural firms is expected to continue to evolve. In this chapter, we'll explore the emerging trends and technologies in BIM, the potential impact of BIM on the architecture industry, and the opportunities and challenges for architectural firms.

9.1. Emerging Trends and Technologies in BIM

9.1.1.   Cloud-Based Collaboration: Cloud-based collaboration is becoming increasingly popular as a way to enhance communication and collaboration between project teams. With cloud-based BIM, team members can work on the same project from different locations and share project information and data in real-time.

9.1.2.   Virtual and Augmented Reality: Virtual and augmented reality technologies are rapidly advancing and are becoming more accessible to architects. These technologies enable architects to create immersive experiences that allow clients to visualize and experience their designs before construction begins.

9.1.3.   Generative Design: Generative design is an emerging technology that uses algorithms to generate design options based on user-defined parameters. This technology can help architects to quickly generate and evaluate design options, saving time and resources.

9.1.4.   Artificial Intelligence (AI): AI has the potential to transform the way architects work by automating repetitive tasks and providing insights that can inform design decisions. AI-powered tools can analyze data from BIM models to identify design inefficiencies and suggest improvements.

9.2. Potential Impact of BIM on the Architecture Industry

BIM has the potential to significantly impact the architecture industry in several ways:

9.2.1.   Improved Collaboration: BIM facilitates collaboration between project team members, resulting in more efficient communication, fewer errors, and better project outcomes.

9.2.2.   Increased Efficiency: BIM enables architects to streamline their workflows, automate repetitive tasks, and reduce errors, resulting in increased efficiency and productivity.

9.2.3.   Cost Savings: BIM can help architects to identify design inefficiencies and reduce waste, resulting in cost savings for clients.

9.2.4.   Enhanced Sustainability: BIM can be used to analyze and optimize building performance, resulting in more sustainable and energy-efficient designs.

9.3. Opportunities and Challenges for Architectural Firms

While the benefits of BIM are clear, there are also challenges that architectural firms may face when implementing BIM:

9.3.1.   Training and Education: BIM requires specialized training and education, which can be costly and time-consuming for firms to provide.

9.3.2. Cost of Software and Hardware: BIM software and hardware can be expensive, particularly for small firms with limited budgets.

9.3.3. Data Management: BIM generates large amounts of data, which can be difficult to manage and organize effectively.

9.3.4. Legal and Contractual Issues: The use of BIM can raise legal and contractual issues that firms must address, such as ownership of BIM data and liability for errors.

9.4. Integration With Other Management Software

9.4.1. Jet.Build: A New Approach to Project Management:

Adam Stark, co-founder of Jet.Build, explains how the software supports BIM workflows in architectural firms, construction companies, and facility management. According to Stark, Jet functions as the backbone for site operations, administrative oversight for projects, and asset management. Jet.Build's integrations with BIM allow the company to focus on the operations side of development and construction, while BIM focuses on the technical side. This collaboration between BIM and Jet is an optimal means of development and construction management.

Jet.Build, being a newly built software/ technology, offers flexible API endpoints for robust customizable integration capabilities with other BIM software commonly used in the industry. According to Stark, features like drawing management and RFIs are great connectivity points with BIM. Jet can function as the front-facing operations process product while the BIM technology acts as the feed for technical changes and updates.

Regarding the future of BIM, Stark predicts that the evolution of BIM will begin with more accessibility to the technology via newer companies that are enabling cost-effective price points for more design teams, builders, and construction professionals. With wider adoption, the evolution of the technology will enable far more precise pre-construction phases that, naturally, produce better efficiency with improvements on successful on-time and on-budget project delivery. Jet. Build has initiated this exact dynamic via its intuitive-yet-robust ERP construction and development management platform at a cost-effective rate.

Jet.Build prioritizes innovation and staying at the forefront of technology trends in the AEC industry. The company's core product is constantly updated to meet today's technology innovations, and they can update, refine, and implement at a pace that is unattainable for legacy companies. The vision for Jet is to be the real estate industry's "smartphone," enabling project stakeholders to integrate their AI, VR/AR, metaverse, and other essential digital operations into Jet. Jet centralizes all teams and all data.

9.4.2. Buildertrend: A Comprehensive Construction Management Solution:

Buildertrend is a cloud-based construction

management software that has been in the industry for nearly two decades, offering comprehensive project management solutions to architectural firms, construction companies, and home builders.

The software supports BIM workflows by integrating with popular BIM software in the industry, enabling users to manage projects and collaborate with team members more efficiently. According to the company, Buildertrend helps users streamline their workflows, increase efficiency, and reduce errors. With over 1 million construction professionals served and 2 million projects completed in the platform, Buildertrend has become the leader of residential construction management platforms.

In conclusion, the future of BIM in architectural firms is promising. Emerging trends and technologies such as cloud-based collaboration, virtual and augmented reality, generative design, and artificial intelligence are expected to transform the way architects work. While there are challenges to implementing BIM, the potential benefits, including improved collaboration, increased efficiency, cost savings, and enhanced sustainability, make it a worthwhile investment for architectural firms.

Figure 17:
HP WMR headset, image by photographer Laurens Derks.

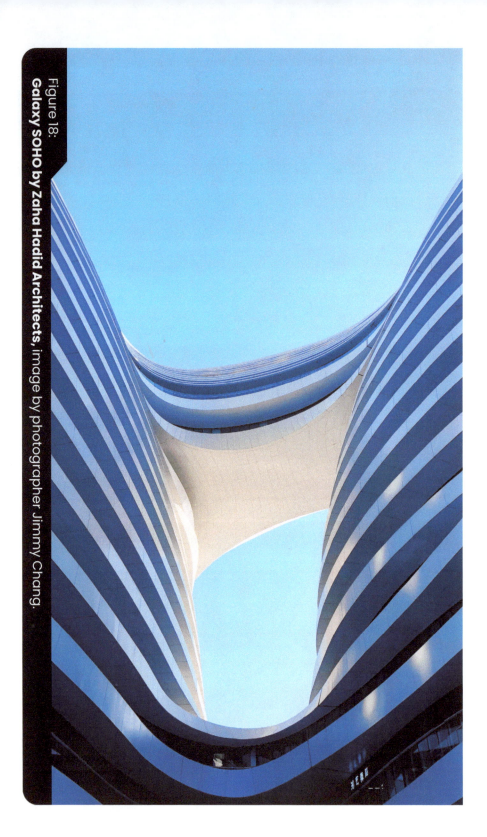

Figure 18:
Galaxy SOHO by Zaha Hadid Architects, image by photographer Jimmy Chang.

Conclusion

Conclusion

In conclusion, implementing BIM in your architectural firm can be a challenging process, but it's worth the effort. By adopting BIM, you can enhance collaboration and communication, reduce errors and rework, and improve the overall efficiency of your projects.

We hope that this guide has provided you with a clear roadmap to implementing BIM in your firm. Remember to assess your needs and resources, develop a BIM execution plan, choose the right software and hardware, train your staff, establish BIM standards and guidelines, and implement best practices for project management.

As a BIM consultancy business, we are committed to helping architectural firms like yours successfully adopt BIM. If you have any questions or would like to learn more about how we can assist you in your BIM implementation journey, please do not hesitate to contact us.

Thank you for considering this guide as a valuable resource. We hope it will inspire you to take the first step towards implementing BIM in your firm and enjoy the many benefits it offers.

Figure 19:
One Thousand Museum by Zaha Hadid Architects, image by photographer Ussama Azam.

Figure 20:
Antwerp Port House by Zaha Hadid Architects, image by photographer Claudia Lorusso.

Selected Bibliography

Selected Bibliography

"3D-4D Building Information Modeling." n.d. Accessed April 23, 2023. https://www.gsa.gov/real-estate/design-and-construction/3d4d-building-information-modeling.

Abbas, Ali, Zia Din, and Rizwan Farooqui. 2016. "Integration of BIM in Construction Management Education: An Overview of Pakistani Engineering Universities." Procedia Engineering 145 (December): 151–57. https://doi.org/10.1016/j.proeng.2016.04.034.

Bukunova, O, and A Bukunov. 2021. "Building Information Modeling for Sustainable Construction." IOP Conference Series: Materials Science and Engineering 1079 (March): 032080. https://doi.org/10.1088/1757-899X/1079/3/032080.

Creative, Michael Maddison-Maddison. n.d. "NBS | Digital Construction Survey 2021 | Introduction." NBS | Digital Construction Survey 2021. Accessed April 22, 2023. https://www.thenbs.com/dcr2021.

Deutsch, Randy. 2011. BIM and Integrated Design: Strategies for Architectural Firms. 1st ed. Hoboken,N.J: Wiley.

Eastman, Charles M., Paul M. Teicholz, Rafael Sacks, and Ghang Lee. 2018. BIM Handbook: A Guide to Building Information Modeling for Owners, Managers, Designers, Engineers and Contractors. Third edition. Hoboken, New Jersey: Wiley.

Garber, Richard. 2014. BIM Design: Realising the Creative Potential of Building Information Modelling. Chichester, West Sussex, United Kingdom: Wiley.

Gu, Ning, and Kerry London. 2010. "Understanding

and Facilitating BIM Adoption in the AEC Industry." Automation in Construction, The role of VR and BIM to manage the construction and design processes, 19 (8): 988–99. https://doi.org/10.1016/j.autcon.2010.09.002.

Hardin, Brad, and Dave McCool. 2015. BIM and Construction Management: Proven Tools, Methods, and Workflows. Second edition. Indianapolis, Indiana: Sybex, a Wiley brand.

Ingram, Jonathan. 2020. Understanding BIM: The Past, Present and Future. London; New York: Routledge,Taylor & Francis Group.

International Organization for Standardization. 2018a. "ISO 19650-1:2018." https://www.iso.org/standard/68078.html.

———. 2018b. "ISO 19650-2:2018." https://www.iso.org/standard/68080.html.

———. 2020a. "ISO 19650-3:2020." https://www.iso.org/standard/75109.html.

———. 2020b. "ISO 19650-5:2020." https://www.iso.org/standard/74206.html.

———. 2022. "ISO 19650-4:2022." https://www.iso.org/standard/78246.html.

Jernigan, Finith E. 2007. Big BIM, Little Bim: The Practical Approach to Building Information Modeling: Integrated Practice Done the Right Way! 1st ed. Salisbury, Md: 4Site Press.

Jones, Stephen, and Berstein Harvey. 2012. "The Business Value of BIM in North America: Multi-Year Trend Analysis and User Ratings (2007-2012)." https://damassets.autodesk.net/content/dam/autodesk/www/solutions/

building-information-modeling/bim-value/mhc-business-value-of-bim-in-north-america.pdf.

Kensek, Karen M. 2014. Building Information Modeling. First edition. PocketArchitecture : Technical Design Series. London ; New York: Routledge, Taylor & Francis Group.

Kensek, Karen M., and Douglas E. Noble, eds. 2014. Building Information Modeling: BIM in Current and Future Practice. Hoboken, New Jersey: Wiley.

Krygiel, Eddy, and Brad Nies. 2008. Green BIM: Successful Sustainable Design with Building Information Modeling. Sybex Serious Skills. Indianapolis, Ind: Wiley Pub.

Kymmell, Willem. 2008. Building Information Modeling: Planning and Managing Construction Projects with 4D CAD and Simulations. McGraw-Hill Construction Series. New York: McGraw-Hill.

Leite, Fernanda L. 2020. BIM for Design Coordination: A Virtual Design and Construction Guide for Designers, General Contractors, and MEP Subcontractors. First edition. Hoboken, New Jersey: Wiley.

Lévy, François. 2012. BIM in Small-Scale Sustainable Design. Hoboken, N.J: Wiley.

———. 2019. BIM for Design Firms: Data Rich Architecture at Small and Medium Scales. Hoboken, NJ: Wiley.

Morlhon, Romain, Robert Pellerin, and Mario Bourgault. 2014. "Building Information Modeling Implementation through Maturity Evaluation and Critical Success Factors Management." Procedia Technology, CENTERIS 2014 - Conference on ENTERprise Information Systems / ProjMAN 2014 - International Conference on Project MANagement / HCIST 2014 - International Conference on Health and Social Care Information Systems and Technologies, 16 (January): 1126–34. https://doi.org/10.1016/j.protcy.2014.10.127.

Norbert W. Young Jr, Stephen A. Jones, Harvey M. Bernstein, and John E. Gudgel. 2009. "The Business Value of Bim: Getting Building Information Modeling To The Bottom Line | PDF | Building Information Modeling | Return On Investment."

Smith, Dana K., and Michael Tardif. 2009. Building Information Modeling: A Strategic Implementation Guide for Architects, Engineers, Constructors, and Real Estate Asset Managers. Hoboken, N.J: Wiley.

Stephen A. Jones and Harvey M. Bernstein. 2014. "The Business Value of BIM for Construction in Major Global Markets: How Contractors Around the World Are Driving Innovation With Building Information Modeling." https://www.academia.edu/27756523/The_Business_Value_of_BIM_for_Construction_in_Major_Global_Markets_How_Contractors_Around_the_World_Are_Driving_Innovation_With_Building_Information_Modeling.

Succar, Bilal. 2009a. "Building Information Modelling Framework: A Research and Delivery Foundation for Industry Stakeholders." Automation in Construction 18 (3): 357–75. https://doi.org/10.1016/j.autcon.2008.10.003.

———. 2009b. "Building Information Modelling Framework: A Research and Delivery Foundation for Industry Stakeholders." Automation in Construction 18 (3): 357–75. https://doi.org/10.1016/j.autcon.2008.10.003.

Succar, Bilal, and Mohamad Kassem. 2015. "Macro-BIM Adoption: Conceptual Structures." Automation in Construction 57 (September): 64–79. https://doi.org/10.1016/j.autcon.2015.04.018.

Tezel, Algan, Martin Taggart, Lauri Koskela, Patrícia Tzortzopoulos, John Hanahoe, and Mark Kelly. 2020. "Lean Construction and BIM in Small and Medium-Sized Enterprises (SMEs) in Construction: A Systematic Literature Review." Canadian Journal of Civil Engineering 47 (February): 186–201. https://doi.org/10.1139/cjce-2018-0408.

"UK BIM Framework – BIM Standards, Guides & Resources." 2019. October 2, 2019. https://www.ukbimframework.org/.

Underwood, Jason, and Umit Isikdag, eds. 2010. Handbook of Research on Building Information Modeling and Construction Informatics: Concepts and Technologies. Hershey, PA: Information Science Reference.

"U.S. National BIM Program | National Institute of Building Sciences." n.d. Accessed April 22, 2023. https://www.nibs.org/usbimprogram.

"Welcome to the National BIM Standard - United States | National BIM Standard - United States." n.d. Accessed April 22, 2023. https://www.nationalbimstandard.org/.

Weygant, Robert S. 2011. BIM Content Development: Standards, Strategies, and Best Practices. Hoboken, N.J: Wiley.

Wing, Eric. 2019. Revit 2020 for Architecture: No Experience Required. John Wiley & Sons.

Wong, Kam-din, and Qing Fan. 2013. "Building Information Modelling (BIM) for Sustainable Building Design." Facilities 31 (February). https://doi.org/10.1108/02632771311299412.

Appendix A: Most Used BIM Software

Appendix A: Most Used BIM Software

In this chapter, we will introduce you to the most commonly used BIM software in the AEC industry. Each software has its unique features and functionalities that cater to the different needs of architectural firms.

Software 1: **Revit**
Developer: Autodesk

Description: Revit is a widely used BIM software that allows architects and designers to create 3D models with precision and accuracy. It offers tools for design, documentation, visualization, and collaboration.

Software 2: **Navisworks**
Developer: Autodesk

Description: Navisworks is a BIM software that provides tools for managing and coordinating building models from different disciplines. It offers features such as clash detection, construction simulation, and project review.

Software 3: **Archicad**
Developer: Graphisoft

Description: Archicad is another popular BIM software that enables architects to create detailed 3D models with BIM data. It offers features such as intelligent building materials, parametric components, and collaboration tools.

Software 4: **OpenBuildings Designer**
Developer: Bentley Systems

Description: OpenBuildings Designer is a BIM software that enables architects and engineers to design and simulate building projects from conception to completion. It provides advanced modeling tools, real-time visualization capabilities, and data management features to help streamline the design process and improve collaboration among project stakeholders. OpenBuildings Designer also supports interoperability with other software platforms, making it a versatile and powerful tool for architectural firms.

Software 5: **Tekla Structures**
Developer: Trimble Inc.

Description: Tekla Structures is a BIM software that is widely used in the construction industry for creating detailed models of steel and concrete structures. It offers tools for detailing, fabrication, and construction planning.

Software 6: **Vectorworks Architect**
Developer: Vectorworks, Inc.

Description: Vectorworks Architect is a BIM software that provides architects with tools for designing, analyzing, and documenting buildings. It offers features such as 3D modeling, parametric design, and collaboration tools.

Software 7: **Blender BIM**
Developer: BlenderBIM Add-on

Description: Blender BIM is a free and open-source BIM software that offers tools for creating 3D models, analyzing structures, and generating documentation. It is suitable for small and medium-sized architectural firms.

Appendix B: Glossary of BIM Keywords and Definitions

Appendix B: Glossary of BIM Keywords and Definitions

In this section, we provide a glossary of BIM keywords and definitions to help readers better understand the concepts and terminology used throughout the book. This glossary is not exhaustive, but it covers some of the most commonly used terms in the BIM industry.

BIM: Building Information Modeling is a digital representation of a building that includes its physical and functional characteristics. It is used to optimize the design, construction, and operation of a building.

BIM execution plan (BEP): A document that outlines the processes, procedures, and protocols that will be used to implement BIM on a specific project or within an organization.

BIM hardware: The physical devices used to run BIM software and process data, such as computers, tablets, and smartphones.

BIM implementation: The process of integrating BIM technology into an organization's workflows and practices.

BIM model: A virtual representation of a building or infrastructure project that includes its geometry, properties, and other data.

BIM project management: The practice of managing BIM projects, including planning, budgeting, and resource allocation.

BIM software: Computer programs used to create, modify, and manage BIM models, such as Autodesk Revit, Bentley Systems MicroStation, and Trimble SketchUp.

BIM standards and guidelines: Guidelines and specifications for the use of BIM software and processes within an organization or industry.

Centralized database: A single repository of data used by multiple users or systems, often used in BIM projects to ensure consistency and accuracy of information.

Clash detection: A BIM process that involves checking for conflicts or inconsistencies between different building elements, systems, or components in a virtual model before construction.

Integrated project delivery (IPD): A project delivery method that involves close collaboration and integration of all project stakeholders, including the owner, architect, contractor, and engineer, from the early stages of design to project completion.

Level of development matrix (LOD): A tool for defining and clarifying the level of development and detail required for each building element or system in a BIM model.

Level of detail (LOD): A standard that defines the level of detail and accuracy of BIM elements at different stages of a project.

On-the-job training: Training provided to employees while they are working on a job, often used in BIM implementation to help users develop the necessary skills and knowledge.

Parametric design: A design approach that uses mathematical algorithms and parameters to create and modify 3D models and drawings.

Point cloud: A collection of points in a 3D space that represents the geometry of a physical object or space. It is often used to create BIM models from laser scans or photogrammetry.

Quantity takeoff: A BIM process of extracting and measuring the quantities of materials and components from a BIM model for estimating and cost control purposes.

Shared parameters: Custom parameters that are defined and shared across different BIM elements in a model. They enable consistent and accurate data management and analysis.

Uniclass: A classification system used in the UK construction industry to organize and manage BIM data.

Workset: A feature in BIM software that enables users to control the visibility and editing of different elements in a shared BIM model. It is often used to manage large and complex projects.

By referring to this glossary, readers can gain a better understanding of BIM-related concepts and terminology used in the book.

Ready to Revolutionize Your BIM Workflow?

Ready to Revolutionize Your BIM Workflow?

Contact D&B Emerging Tech Now!

If you are an architecture firm looking to enhance your BIM workflows and achieve project success, look no further than **D&B** Emerging Tech. With almost three decades of experience in architecture and construction, we have the expertise to deliver exceptional BIM services tailored to your project needs. Our team of experts is dedicated to staying at the forefront of BIM innovation and sharing our knowledge with others in the industry.

Visit our website at *https://dandb.tech* to learn more about our services and expertise, and how we can help you achieve your project goals. Contact us today to schedule a consultation and take the first step towards transforming your projects with BIM. Let us be your partner in innovation, research, and technology.

Our BIM Services

BIM Management And Implementation
BIM Project And Object Modeling
BIM Templates And Documentation
BIM Coordination And Collaboration
BIM Training And Education
BIM Analysis And Simulation
BIM Project Costing And Scheduling
BIM Client Assessment
BIM Visualization And Rendering
BIM Digital Fabrication
BIM Virtual Reality
BIM Artificial Intelligence

Join Archi-Tech Network (ATN) for Comprehensive Online BIM/Revit Courses!

As an architecture professional, you know how important it is to stay up-to-date with the latest BIM software and technologies. That's where Archi-Tech Network (ATN) comes in. We have partnered with them to offer their comprehensive online courses to our clients. ATN's BIM/Revit courses cover everything from basic concepts to advanced techniques, giving you the knowledge and skills you need in professional practice as an architect.

ATN's BIM/Revit courses are designed and taught by experienced architects and BIM experts, who work in the world's leading architectural firms. They provide flexible online learning options that fit your schedule, so you can learn at your own pace and convenience. The Netflix of computational design!

Visit their website at *https://archi-tech.network* to learn more about their course content, pricing, and enrollment options. You can also reach out to us for corporate packages to get your whole staff trained online, with everyone learning at their own pace.

About D&B Emerging Tech

About D&B Emerging Tech

D&B Emerging Tech is a design technology company, and the future of the AEC industry.

With 300+ projects completed, 28+ years experience, and global team in 10+ countries, our sister company **D&B** Ltd is now venturing into innovative design technology services that help clients achieve their goals. Our team of architects, developers, and specialists use the latest technologies to deliver exceptional results.

Our team comprises specialists who are passionate about leveraging the latest technologies to improve project outcomes. At **D&B** Emerging Tech, we believe that BIM is the future of the AEC industry, and we are committed to providing exceptional services that enable our clients to achieve their project goals. We plan to become a leading provider of BIM services, having successfully completed numerous architectural and construction projects, and therefore understanding the opportunities and challenges.

We offer a wide range of BIM related services, including management and coordination, training, research, documentation, BIM object modeling, analysis, costing, visualization, virtual reality, 3d scanning, digital fabrication, AI services and more. We are committed to staying at the forefront of BIM innovation and sharing our knowledge with others in the industry.

For more information about **D&B** Emerging Tech please visit our website at *https://dandb.tech*. And for those seeking to enhance their BIM workflows, we hope that our book, *BIM FOR ARCHITECTURAL FIRMS: A Short Introduction,* serves as a valuable resource.

About Editor

About Editor

Faisal U-K is an Archi-preneur, Superuser, Architectural Designer, Meta-Architect, Design Technologist, BIM Specialist, Researcher, Educator, Author and Podcaster. He currently serves as the CEO of **D&B** Emerging Tech and Design Technology Manager at **D&B** Ltd. He is also the BIM Manager at ATO Architects, Co-Founder of Archi-Tech Network (ATN), and Co-Founder of ILLUSORR, as well as a Founding Principal Member of The Metaverse Standards Forum.

Contact

Faisal U-K,

CEO, **D&B** Emerging Tech

faisaluk@dandb.tech

https://dandb.tech

www.ingramcontent.com/pod-product-compliance
Lightning Source LLC
LaVergne TN
LVHW072050060326
832903LV00054B/383